Nature
INTERRUPTED
The Science of **Environmental Chain Reactions**

by Darlene R. Stille

Content Adviser:
Clarence L. Lehman, Ph.D., Adjunct Professor,
Department of Ecology, Evolution, and Behavior,
University of Minnesota

Science Adviser:
Terrence E. Young Jr., M.Ed., M.L.S.,
Jefferson Parish (Louisiana) Public School System

Reading Adviser:
Rosemary G. Palmer, Ph.D.,
Department of Literacy, College of Education,
Boise State University

Compass Point Books • 151 Good Counsel Drive, P. O. Box 669 • Mankato, MN 56002-0669

Library of Congress Cataloging-in-Publication Data
Stille, Darlene R.
  Nature interrupted : the science of environmental chain reactions / by Darlene Stille.
     p. cm. — (Headline Science)
  Includes bibliographical references and index.
  ISBN 978-0-7565-3949-8 (library binding)
  ISBN 978-0-7565-3950-4 (paperback)
1. Environmental chemistry—Juvenile literature. 2. Chemical reaction,
Conditions and laws of—Juvenile literature. I. Title. II. Series.
  TD193.S75 2008
  577.27—dc22   2008007282

Editor: Jennifer VanVoorst
Designers: Ellen Schofield and Ashlee Suker
Page Production: Ashlee Suker
Photo Researcher: Svetlana Zhurkin
Cartographer: XNR Productions, Inc.
Illustrator: Eric Hoffmann

Art Director: LuAnn Ascheman-Adams
Creative Director: Keith Griffin
Editorial Director: Nick Healy
Managing Editor: Catherine Neitge

Photographs ©: Joseph Luoman/iStockphoto, cover (bottom), 24; Stacey Newman/iStockphoto, cover (inset, left),
29; YinYang/iStockphoto, cover (inset, middle), 41; Viktor Balabanov/iStockphoto, cover (inset, right), 28; Robert
Kirk/iStockphoto, 5; Gregory Donald Horler/Shutterstock, 7; Ewen Cameron/iStockphoto, 8; kaaja/iStockphoto, 9;
Geoff Whiting/iStockphoto, 11; Jeremy Sterk/iStockphoto, 13; Willi Schmitz/iStockphoto, 14; Francisco Romero/
iStockphoto, 16; David Pedre/iStockphoto, 17; U.S. Fish and Wildlife Service, 19; Oksana Perkins/iStockphoto, 20;
An Nguyen/Shutterstock, 21; AP Photo/Jeff Barnard, 22; Gary Gaugler/Visuals Unlimited, 25; Kimberly White/
Getty Images, 27; Jaap Hart/iStockphoto, 31; Lidian Neeleman/iStockphoto, 33; David Dohnal/Shutterstock, 34;
NOAA Climate Program Office, NABOS 2006 Expedition, photo by Mike Dunn, 35; Richard Simpkins/iStockphoto,
36; Ralph125/iStockphoto, 37; Christopher Arndt/iStockphoto, 38; Brazil2/iStockphoto, 40; Grafissimo/iStock-
photo, 43.

Visit Compass Point Books on the Internet at *www.compasspointbooks.com*
or e-mail your request to *custserv@compasspointbooks.com*

SLUDGE RECYCLING SENDS ANTISEPTIC SOAP INGREDIENT TO AGRICULTURE

>>> Johns Hopkins Bloomberg School of Public Health
April 26, 2006

Researchers at the Johns Hopkins Bloomberg School of Public Health measured levels of an antibacterial hand soap ingredient, triclocarban, as it passed through a wastewater treatment facility. They determined that approximately 75 percent of the ingredient washed down the drain by consumers persists during waste-water treatment and accumulates in municipal sludge, which later is used as fertilizer for crops. Their findings are presented in a study appearing in the online and print editions of the journal *Environmental Science & Technology*. More studies are under way to determine if triclocarban, which is toxic when ingested, can migrate from sludge into foods, thereby potentially posing a human health risk.

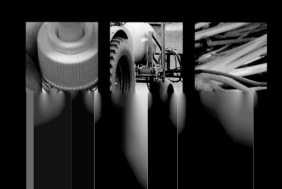

So you are trying to do the right thing by washing your hands frequently. You know that hand washing is the best way to keep colds, flu, and other diseases caused by germs from spreading. For good measure, you use a soap that you believe has extra germ-killing power. Now some scientists suspect that your good intentions could be causing pollution.

NOW YOU KNOW

Researchers say that washing with antibacterial soap is no more effective at preventing the spread of infection than washing with ordinary soap and water.

Seemingly innocent everyday behaviors such as washing your hands with antibacterial soap can have a negative impact on the environment.

News changes every minute, and readers need access to the latest information to keep current. Here are a few key search terms to help you locate up-to-the-minute environmental chain reactions headlines:

acid rain

alien species

Bt corn

eutrophication

fertilizer runoff

genetically altered foods

global warming

habitat fragmentation

mercury pollution

oil spill

We might think that only "bad" activities, such as dumping chemical wastes, can harm the environment. Sometimes, however, an environmental chain reaction starts with a good idea. It might start with a plan to get rid of disease-causing insects or to fertilize soil to produce crops that can feed more people. It could start in your backyard with a chemical to get rid of dandelions. It often takes just one small action to have far-reaching effects.

EVERYDAY CHAIN REACTIONS

Small changes in the environment can be difficult to see. We might not notice changes until an entire plant or animal species disappears. We might not pay attention until there is a threat to our health. It is much easier to see chain reactions in everyday life. Those everyday chain reactions involve the same types of steps as an environmental chain reaction.

The fertilizer choices farmers make can have an effect on many aspects of the environment, from the soil to water quality.

Suppose there was a big pileup of vehicles on an interstate highway. It could have started with one car that had faulty brakes. The brakes would not slow the car fast enough to avoid hitting the car in front. One car crashes into another. Then suppose a tanker truck carrying liquid chlorine crashes into the pileup of cars and explodes. The chlorine vaporizes into a gas. It spreads as a poisonous cloud over the entire area, killing hundreds of people. The chain reaction that led to this highway disaster could have been avoided if the driver of the first car had only had the brakes checked and fixed. The same is true for preventing many environmental chain reactions.

LOOKING FOR THE FIRST LINK

Research scientists watch for the first link in an environmental chain reaction. They are on the lookout for early signs of environmental threats. The scientists who studied the sludge from a wastewater treatment plant, for example, knew that the chemi-

cal triclocarban in antibacterial soap does not break down easily. They had found that the chemical was already polluting water taken from rivers and streams. Would fertilizer made from the sludge make the pollution worse? To find out, they took samples from a large water treatment plant for several

Wastewater is treated in large, aboveground tanks at water processing plants.

weeks. They analyzed how much triclocarban was in water coming into the plant. Then they analyzed how much of the chemical was in the sludge going out. In that way, they discovered that three-fourths of it remained. More studies are needed to find out all about triclocarban's journey through water and soil. The scientists suspect that it could end up in plant roots from soil treated with fertilizer made from the sludge.

All over the world, scientists are on the alert for clues that signal environmental danger. Their ideal goal would be to stop the first link in a harmful environmental chain reaction from ever forming.

Root vegetables such as carrots could be tainted by chemicals such as triclocarban if the soil in which they are grown is treated with fertilizer made from polluted wastewater.

HABITAT DESTRUCTION MAY WIPE OUT MONARCH BUTTERFLY MIGRATION

>> Science Daily
April 5, 2008

Intense deforestation in Mexico could ruin one of North America's most celebrated natural wonders—the mysterious 3,000-mile migration of the monarch butterfly. According to a University of Kansas researcher, the astonishing migration may collapse rapidly without urgent action to end devastation of the butterfly's vital sources of food and shelter. ...

[The] Monarch Biosphere Reserve ... in central Mexico ... is the winter home for millions of migrating butterflies from across the continent. In spite of its protected status, the isolated reserve is suffering from illegal logging. ... Over the past two winters, millions of monarchs have died from exposure to wind and cold temperatures in clear-cut areas.

Environmental chain reactions can affect an area as large as the whole planet or as small as a pond in a city park. All chain reactions happen because of how Earth and everything on it works. Earth is made up of interacting parts that connect together and affect one another. Scientists classify, or group, interacting areas of Earth into biomes and ecosystems. To understand how environmental chain reactions can damage the environment, it is important to understand what biomes and ecosystems are and how they work.

BIOMES

Biomes are major life zones covering millions of square miles. Biologists classify biomes by the major types of plants that grow there. Grasses grow in a grassland biome. A conifer-

Cactuses grow in the hot, dry desert biome.

ous forest biome contains largely pines, firs, and other cone-bearing trees. A temperate deciduous biome contains oaks, maples, elms, and other leafy trees that grow in a climate with four seasons.

Climate is mainly what determines the different kinds of biomes. The tundra biome, where lichens, moss, and small plants grow, lies toward the Arctic Circle, where the climate is cold. Tropical rain forests lie near the equator, where the climate is wet and warm. Desert biomes exist where there is little rainfall. There are also freshwater and saltwater biomes.

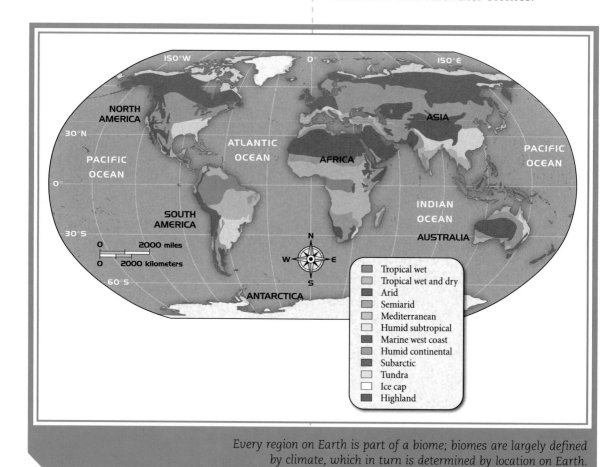

Every region on Earth is part of a biome; biomes are largely defined by climate, which in turn is determined by location on Earth.

A biome can contain many kinds of ecosystems, from a stream or a lake to a meadow or woodland.

ECOSYSTEMS AND ENERGY FLOW

Ecosystems are all the living things in particular areas and all the nonliving things they interact with. An ecosystem contains many habitats. A habitat is an area within an ecosystem where a population—a group of the same kind of organisms—lives at the same time.

An ecosystem can be any size, from a few acres to hundreds of square

A pond ecosystem supports a variety of living things, such as birds, fish, insects, trees, grasses, and many other organisms.

miles. An ecosystem's nonliving parts include rocks and soil, precipitation, temperature, and sunlight. The living parts are plants, animals, and decomposers, such as fungi and bacteria. Ecologists study how all the living and nonliving parts work together to keep the ecosystem in balance. They also study how environmental chain reactions upset the balance.

One way in which all the parts work together is through the flow of energy. Energy flows from one organism to another through a food web. A food web consists of many food chains. The food web begins with energy from sunlight. Green plants and some other organisms use sunlight along with water and carbon dioxide in the air, plus small amounts of material from the soil, to make their own food.

The next level of energy flow in a food web involves animals that eat plants. Then come animals that eat other animals and animals that eat either animals or

Cows have an intermediate position in the food web: They eat grass but in turn are eaten by many people.

plants. When plants, animals, and other organisms die, decomposers such as bacteria break down the dead material. Eventually the chemicals in the dead organisms return either to the soil or become part of a chemical cycle.

PLANETWIDE CYCLES

Water, carbon dioxide, and nitrogen cycle through ecosystems and biomes. These cycles involve the whole planet. In the water cycle, moisture forms clouds in the atmosphere. Droplets fall to Earth as rain or other precipitation. Rainwater flows downhill into creeks that join rivers and lakes, and eventually flows into the ocean. Rainwater carries chemicals that it has picked up from the land on its way. Heat from the sun evaporates ocean water, and clouds form. From clouds, the water eventually drops back to Earth as precipitation.

The carbon cycle involves atoms of the element carbon. Every living thing contains carbon atoms. Carbon atoms are recycled over and over

again. The carbon cycle has two parts: the biological carbon cycle and the geological carbon cycle. In the biological carbon cycle, plants take in carbon dioxide and water and give off oxygen as a waste product. Animals breathe in the oxygen and use it to burn food for energy. Animals then breathe out carbon dioxide and water as waste products. Plants recycle the carbon dioxide to produce more food.

The geological carbon cycle has many more parts. Carbon is "locked

NOW YOU KNOW

In 2007, the state of Georgia had a severe drought while the United Kingdom experienced flooding. There can be varying amounts of water in different places at different times. However, Earth's water cycle ensures that Earth will have the same total amount of water in the future as it had in the past.

With their many plants and animals, rain forests are part of both the biological and geological carbon cycles.

up" in the trees of vast forests, for example. It is locked up in coal, oil, and other fossil fuels that formed from living organisms that died millions of years ago. It is locked up in ocean water and in a rock called limestone that formed from the shells of dead sea creatures. It is also locked up in the vast coral reefs of the oceans.

The nitrogen cycle is also important to life, because living things need atoms of this chemical element. The cycle begins with microscopic organisms called nitrogen-fixing bacteria.

These bacteria attach to plants called legumes and take nitrogen gas out of the air. They turn the gas into a form that plants can take up from the soil. In this way, nitrogen becomes a kind of natural fertilizer. Nitrogen atoms then pass through the food web to animals, which release nitrogen in waste products. When plants and animals die, decomposers break down their remains and release the nitrogen back into the cycle. ◄

Nitrogen-fixing bacteria exist in the roots of legumes such as peanuts and return nitrogen to the soil.

SHRIMPY INVADERS

>>> Science News for Kids
January 17, 2007

A new type of shrimplike crustacean has appeared in the Great Lakes, and that's not necessarily a good thing.

These crustaceans, called mysid shrimp, normally live in rivers near the western coast of the Caspian Sea in Eastern Europe. In November, researchers from the National Oceanic and Atmospheric Administration (NOAA) found invading mysid shrimp in a channel in Lake Michigan. Now, NOAA reports that large numbers of the animal ... are living in southeastern Lake Ontario. ...

Mysid shrimp devour microscopic animals, which many young fish in the Great Lakes also eat. A heavy dose of new competition for food may harm fish populations.

Tiny shrimp invading the Great Lakes could throw the food web out of balance. A balanced ecosystem has predators—animals that eat other animals. It also has prey—animals that are eaten by predators. Adding or removing either prey or predators sets off an environmental chain reaction in the ecosystem's food web. Alien invaders have done this before.

A tiny crustacean called the zebra mussel appeared in the Great Lakes near Detroit, Michigan, in 1988. A ship carried the mussel from Russia in water inside its hull. The crew pumped the water into Lake Erie as part of cleaning the ship. The zebra mussels reproduced rapidly. By 2000, they had invaded all the Great Lakes and nearby rivers.

The mussels greatly changed water ecosystems. Each mussel sucks in about a gallon (3.8 liters) of water a day. It takes particles of food from the water and leaves little for fish larvae or other tiny animals to eat. Zebra mussels also attach to solid surfaces such as clamshells, boat docks, and pipes that take in drinking water. Clearing clogged water pipes of these mussels has cost lakefront communities about $300 million. A native clam in Lake Erie has almost gone extinct. The

Zebra mussels attach to solid surfaces in lakes, including native mussels.

zebra mussel, however, provides food for other fish such as northern pike and yellow perch. The number of these fish increased. By the early 2000s, more than 1 million zebra mussels per square mile (2.6 square kilometers) lived in certain parts of Lake Erie.

FILLING A NICHE

Alien invaders such as mysid shrimp and zebra mussels set off chain reac-tions because every population in an ecosystem occupies a particular niche. A niche is the role that a population plays in an ecosystem. A niche covers where the population lives, what individuals in the population eat, who their natural enemies are, what range of temperatures they can live in, how much water they need, whether the population migrates and when, and how it breeds.

Grizzly bears and salmon occupy different niches within an ecosystem.

A population shares an ecosystem with many other populations, and these populations often interact with one another. They have different relationships, such as a predator and prey relationship. Two populations rarely occupy the same niche, because they must compete for food and other resources. Zebra mussels and fish larvae compete for food in an ecosystem. Because they are more efficient feeders, the zebra mussels win.

CHAIN REACTIONS IN HABITATS

Environmental chain reactions can lead to the extinction of a species. Losing a species, in turn, can lead to more chain reactions in an ecosystem. Natural predators of whitetail deer, for example, have disappeared from rural and suburban ecosystems. Without predators, the deer population has exploded. Large numbers of deer can destroy orchards and gardens. A major

Because of a series of environmental chain reactions, deer and other wild animals are finding their way into the suburbs.

cause of species extinction in the modern world is habitat destruction. Habitat destruction can occur on land, in freshwater lakes and rivers, and in the ocean.

For example, building a dam can set off environmental chain reactions in river habitats. Environmentalists in the early 2000s asked that many of the more than 75,000 dams in the United States either be improved to create better water flow or be torn down. A dam blocks the flow of river water, creating a lake, or reservoir, behind the dam. Blocking water flow lowers the water level in the river on the other side of the dam. The shallow river water can become too warm or too salty for the populations that usually live there.

A series of dams on the Rio Grande between Mexico and the United States low-

Dams block the natural flow of water, altering the water's temperature or composition and creating problems for the organisms that depend on it.

ered river water and set off a chain reaction. The water became salty enough to damage crops, kill native species, and even damage plumbing. In addition, pollutants can build up in reservoirs behind the dams. Dams on the Klamath River in Oregon and northern California prevent salmon from swimming up rivers to spawn. In 2007, the federal government ordered the dams to be fixed so that salmon can get over them.

TROPICAL RAIN FOREST DESTRUCTION

Some of the greatest environmental chain reactions of the late 1900s and early 2000s were taking place in tropical rain forests. These forests cover millions of square miles in South America, Southeast Asia, and other parts of the globe. The largest rain forest, the Amazon rain forest in Brazil, covers an area as big as Western Europe.

People cut down the trees for lumber. They also clear rain forest lands to plant crops and build roads.

Scientists study satellite photos to see how much forest has been lost. No one knows for sure, but some environmentalists estimate that an area of forest equal to two football fields is lost every second.

Tropical rain forests are important in the carbon cycle. They take carbon from the atmosphere and store it or use it to make food and give off oxygen. Half of all the species on Earth might live in rain forests. Most of these species have not yet been discovered, including plants that could possibly provide medicines for cancer and other diseases. One out of four modern drugs come from rain forest plants. No one today can predict what environmental chain reactions might occur if all the tropical rain forests are cut down.

Breaking up habitats is another problem. Biologists call this problem habitat fragmentation. Sometimes a habitat gets broken up for different uses. One part of a forest habitat may become a farm and another part a town. On either side of the town and

The destruction of rain forests promises wide-ranging environmental chain reactions that will affect many aspects of our lives.

farm, forest remains. Some species that need large forest areas may not be able to cross the farm and town to reach the other part of the forest. Such species die off. Meanwhile, the number of individuals in a population that can easily adapt to the new situation, such as deer, raccoons, and foxes, greatly increases.

NONLIVING CHAIN REACTIONS

Changes in nonliving parts of an ecosystem can also set off environmental chain reactions. For example, medical researchers were puzzled by outbreaks of plague in New Mexico in the 1990s. Plague is caused by a bacterium, and it can be deadly if not treated with antibiotics. A plague epidemic called the Black Death wiped out one-third of the people in Europe in the 1300s. Plague bacteria live in fleas that in turn live on rats and other rodents. If the fleas reach the skin of humans, the fleas can pass on the bacteria through bites.

Ecologists solved the mystery of why plague showed up in New Mexico. They found that plague outbreaks followed unusually heavy rainfalls. The rainfall increased the number of plants that rodents feed on. At the same time, the number of fleas increased in the wet soil. The increased populations of rodents and the fleas they carried began to spread into new areas. Eventually, the rodents came into contact with people or with their pet cats and dogs. The fleas passed on the bacteria that cause plague.

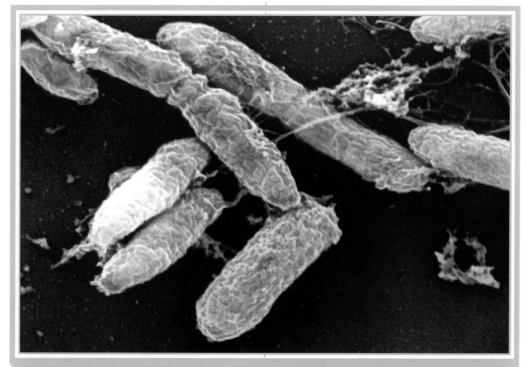

Plague bacteria seen under a microscope

OIL SPILL SPREADS IN SAN FRANCISCO BAY

>>> *The New York Times*
November 10, 2007

Challenged by strong winds and tides, cleanup crews struggled Friday to contain an oil spill spreading in the San Francisco Bay. ...

A thick black film spread over the bay water. The oil coated birds and marine mammals. Rescuers tried to clean the animals off to prevent them from dying. Chemicals in the petroleum, however, can poison fish and other animals that live underwater. Because oil and its toxic chemicals seep into sand and soil along beaches and on the seafloor, it can take a long time for an ecosystem to recover. "The effects of the oil spill could persist for months and possibly years," said Tina Swanson, a fish biologist with the Bay Institute.

Environmental scientists know right away that an oil spill is causing serious problems. However, some problems in water ecosystems are not as easy to see. Too many nutrients, for example, can throw a lake ecosystem totally out of balance. The ecosystem can even be destroyed. Lake Erie was lucky to escape this fate.

By the early 2000s, Lake Erie had come back to life, but in the 1960s, environmentalists had declared the lake "dead." A smelly scum covered the surface. Fish and other animals died off. The "killer" turned out to be laundry detergent. Fertilizers and sewage also added to the problem.

Lake Erie was the victim of a complex environmental chain reaction. The reaction begins when too

A worker attempted to protect the beach from an oil spill in San Francisco Bay in November 2007.

many nutrients get into a lake or stream. The nutrients can come from sewage, factory chemicals, and fertilizers. In Lake Erie, the nutrients came from laundry detergent. At that time, detergents contained chemicals called phosphates, which were good at getting greasy dirt out of clothes. Phosphates contain a chemical element called phosphorus, a plant fertilizer.

Phosphorus began its trip to Lake Erie when water from washing machines poured into sewers. From there, the water went through treatment plants and into the lake. The phosphorus, however, remained in the water.

In the lake, the phosphorus helped plants grow. The lake ecosystem was in balance until the extra fertilizer

Treated water dumped into lakes and streams may not be entirely rid of environmental poisons.

arrived. Suddenly, plants and algae begin to grow out of control. Biologists call this sudden growth an algal bloom. They call the environmental chain reaction this causes eutrophication. When plants and algae die off, bacteria and other decomposers go to work breaking down the dead material. Bacteria use up oxygen in the water, and without enough oxygen, fish die. In a large lake, the lack of oxygen causes "dead zones" where nothing can live. In a small lake, the decayed material can build up so much that the lake ecosystem turns into another kind of ecosystem—a swamp or even dry land.

Help came to Lake Erie after scientists discovered the problem. In the 1970s, U.S. citizens, through their government, banned the use of phosphates in laundry detergents. Slowly,

An algal bloom causes dead zones, depriving fish and other lake creatures of the oxygen they need to survive.

the algae began to die off, and the fish population grew larger. Today the bad smell is gone, and people again can go to the beach and swim in Lake Erie.

TROUBLE IN THE WATER CYCLE

Chemicals that enter the air can cause complex environmental chain reactions in the water cycle. Burning coal gives off chemical particles that turn to acids when they mix with moisture in the air. Eventually the chemicals fall back to Earth as acid rain, snow, or fog. Acid rain can make the water of a lake ecosystem so acidic that it kills off organisms in the lake. On land, acid rain can damage or kill off trees and other plants. A study in 2007 showed that acid rain can weaken the disease-fighting ability even in trees that do not die.

Another dangerous environmental chain reaction involves mercury, the water cycle, and the food web. In 2004, the U.S. government warned against eating too much seafood. The warning said that all fish and shellfish contain some mercury.

Mercury is a toxic chemical that can harm the nervous system and internal organs. In pregnant women, it can damage the growing baby. The chain reaction begins when smokestacks on power plants and factories that burn coal send mercury into the air. Wind and clouds carry the mercury for hundreds, even thousands, of miles. The mercury falls into the ocean as rain or snow. If it falls on land, it can wash into rivers and lakes and then into the sea.

Once mercury gets into the ocean, an environmental chain reaction begins in the food web. Plankton, tiny

NOW YOU KNOW

The water in a lake ecosystem that has been severely damaged by acid rain can be sparkling clear and clean looking because nothing can live in it.

Coal-burning power plants can send mercury into the air, beginning an environmental chain reaction that involves both the water cycle and food webs.

organisms that float near the surface of the sea, take up the mercury. Fish larvae and other small animals eat plankton. Larger fish eat the small marine animals, and these fish are then eaten by bigger fish. Each time a large fish eats a smaller one, the large fish takes in more and more mercury. Eventually, the mercury gets into big predatory fish, such as tuna, at the top of the food web. The more fish the tuna eats, the more mercury it takes into its body.

Fishing boats catch fish and shellfish. The seafood then is sold to restaurants, grocery stores, and canning companies. The environmental chain reaction that began when burning coal gave off mercury ends with mercury in food that people eat.

STUDY DETAILS HOW U.S. COULD CUT 28% OF GREENHOUSE GASES

>>> *The New York Times*
November 30, 2007

The United States could shave as much as 28 percent off the amount of greenhouse gases it emits at fairly modest cost and with only small technology innovations, according to a new report.

A large share of the reductions could come from steps that would more than pay for themselves in lower energy bills for industries and individual consumers, the report said, adding that people should take those steps out of good sense regardless of how worried they might be about climate change.

What does turning on a light or watching television have to do with the global carbon cycle? These activities use electricity, and electricity comes from power plants. Most electric power plants in the United States burn coal to heat water and make steam. The steam drives big machines that make electricity. In addition to other pollutants, burning coal gives off carbon dioxide, the same gas that plants use in making food.

Scientists call carbon dioxide a greenhouse gas. It is part of Earth's atmosphere—a blanket of gases that surrounds the planet. Greenhouse gases in the atmosphere keep Earth warm enough for life. The gases help hold heat that originally came from the sun close to Earth's surface. Like

Certain gases work like the glass panels on a greenhouse to trap heat in Earth's atmosphere, warming the environment.

all the parts that make up Earth's environment, greenhouse gases work well when they are in balance. Since the mid-1800s, however, the amount of carbon dioxide has been growing faster and faster. Scientists fear that the extra carbon dioxide is causing global warming. The warming could eventually melt the ice caps at the North and South Poles. The melting would raise sea levels and cause other climate changes. Severe droughts, for example, could dry up Midwestern farmlands. Hurricanes and other storms could flood cities along the Atlantic coast.

Throughout the history of Earth, changes in temperature have caused changes in biomes. Places that were once tropical swamps became ice-covered wastelands. Changes in rainfall patterns caused rain forest biomes to become desert biomes. Natural changes have set off many environ-

NOW YOU KNOW

Scientists in 2007 reported that human activity sends nearly 9 billion tons (8 billion metric tons) of carbon dioxide into the atmosphere each year, and that amount is increasing.

Global warming is causing severe droughts, drying up lakes and changing temperate biomes into desert ones.

mental chain reactions that gradually changed biomes and ecosystems. Now human activities are setting off environmental chain reactions that could cause very rapid changes on our planet.

THE STEAM ENGINE LINK

The amount of carbon dioxide in the atmosphere began to grow after the steam engine was invented in the 1700s. The steam engine drove machines in factories. Making goods in factories set off the Industrial Revolution. By the mid-1800s, the Industrial Revolution was in full swing all over Europe and the United States. Smoke-stacks on factories poured tons of dirty pollutants into the air, along with invisible carbon dioxide.

Scientists study carbon dioxide in Earth's atmosphere. They send up balloons to take samples of the air. They drill deep into ice and take out long cores. The cores contain bubbles of air trapped in the ice hundreds or thousands of years ago. Scientists then analyze the ice and the bubbles. They

have found that since the mid-1800s, carbon dioxide rapidly increased. By 2000, there was far more carbon dioxide in the atmosphere than there had ever been since humans first inhabited Earth. Much of this excess carbon dioxide went into the atmosphere just

A scientist sawed through an ice core to obtain a sample for analysis.

since the 1950s. Scientists all over the world agree that human activities are putting extra carbon dioxide into the atmosphere. The increase is linked to global warming.

RELEASING ANCIENT CARBON DIOXIDE

The machines of the Industrial Revolution needed energy. The energy came first from coal and then from oil and natural gas. Coal, oil, and natural gas are fossil fuels. They formed mainly from plants that died millions of years ago. Over millions of years, thick layers of mud and rock piled up over the decaying plants. Buried deep in the ground, the plant material slowly turned into coal, oil, and natural gas. The fossil fuels looked very different

Coal is created over millions of years as pressure is naturally applied to decaying plant matter.

from the original plants. However, they still held the carbon that the plants took out of the air to make food millions of years ago.

The need for more fossil fuels grew. After Thomas Edison perfected the incandescent lightbulb in the late 1800s, people wanted electricity in their homes. One electric power plant after another was built. First they all burned coal, but some later burned oil for energy.

Another link in the environmental chain reaction leading to global warming was the automobile. Automobiles became popular in the early 1900s. By the 1950s, almost all U.S. families owned at least one car. Automobiles run on gasoline, which is refined, or made, from oil. Burning gasoline in car engines in the United States alone sends more than 345 million tons (314 million metric tons) of carbon dioxide into the atmosphere each year.

A REVERSE CHAIN REACTION

The good news is that scientists say we can all do something about global warming. Families can start a chain reaction to reverse the amount of carbon dioxide going into the air. Turning off unused appliances and using energy-efficient fluorescent lightbulbs, for example, cuts down on the amount of electric energy your house needs. If every house in a community cut down on energy use, the local power plant

HEADLINE SCIENCE

Emissions from automobiles are a significant contributor to global warming.

would not have to produce as much electricity. Therefore, the power plant would not need to burn as much coal or oil. Burning less fuel would cut down on the carbon dioxide going into the atmosphere.

Researchers are working on new technologies to help coal give off less carbon dioxide. Energy companies are working on solar panels that turn rays from the sun into electricity. They are building windmills that generate electric power. Electric companies are developing ways to capture carbon dioxide given off by their power plants and pump it into underground storage areas. Engineers are trying to make nuclear power plants safer. Inventors are trying to make longer-lasting batteries for providing power to cars. By the early 2000s, some automobile

Wind farms capture the energy of the wind and convert it to electricity; as wind moves across the blades of the windmills, causing them to spin, the motion is transferred to a generator, which creates electricity.

manufacturers were selling hybrid gas-electric cars that get as much as 50 miles per gallon (5.6 liters per 100 km) of gasoline.

GENETICALLY ENGINEERED CORN MAY HARM STREAM ECOSYSTEMS

National Science Foundation
October 10, 2007

A new study indicates that a popular type of genetically engineered corn—called Bt corn—may damage the ecology of streams draining Bt corn fields in ways that have not been previously considered by regulators. The study, which was funded by the National Science Foundation, appears in the Oct. 8 edition of *The Proceedings of the National Academy of Sciences*. This study provides the first evidence that toxins from Bt corn may travel long distances in streams and may harm stream insects that serve as food for fish. These results compound concerns about the ecological impacts of Bt corn raised by previous studies showing that corn-grown toxins harm beneficial insects living in the soil.

Genetic scientists have long dreamed about using genes, the basic unit of heredity, to improve people's lives. Genetic science already produces important drugs such as human insulin to treat people with diabetes. In 1953, scientists learned about DNA, the molecule that genes are made of. Since then, they have discovered ways to alter genes in plants. They can make food plants more nutritious. They can give them the ability to fight off insect pests and thus eliminate the need for chemical fertilizer.

A CHAIN REACTION FROM CORN

The story of Bt corn began when researchers discovered a bacterium that could poison an insect harmful

A sign identified a field of cotton that was a trial site for genetically modified organisms (GMOs).

Today there is increased demand for Bt corn because of corn's importance as a biofuel, a kind of fuel made from crops.

to corn. The bacterium, called *Bacillus thuringiensis* (Bt), had a special gene for making the poison. Genetic engineers in the mid-1990s used a kind of chemical scissors to cut the gene for this toxin out of the bacterium. They used other chemicals to "paste" it into the genes of a corn plant. Sure enough, when harmful insects tried to eat the Bt corn, they were poisoned. Bt corn became very popular. By 2006,

about 35 percent of all corn planted in the United States was Bt corn.

NEW GENE IN AN ECOSYSTEM

Meanwhile, signs of problems began to appear. In 1999, biologists at Cornell University found that pollen from Bt corn could kill monarch butterfly caterpillars. Wind blew the pollen onto milkweed plants near the cornfields.

The caterpillars do not eat corn pollen, but they do eat milkweed. The caterpillars ate the poisonous pollen along with the milkweed plants. In 2007, a study showed that Bt pollen and corn parts could be washed by rain into lakes and streams. Insects called caddisflies died after eating Bt corn pollen. Caddisflies are an important food source for fish and amphibians in water ecosystems. Researchers are watching closely for signs of a new environmental chain reaction.

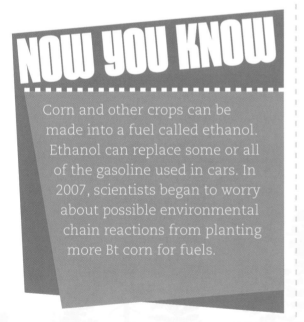

NOW YOU KNOW

Corn and other crops can be made into a fuel called ethanol. Ethanol can replace some or all of the gasoline used in cars. In 2007, scientists began to worry about possible environmental chain reactions from planting more Bt corn for fuels.

MAKING WISE CHOICES

People look to new technology to solve many problems. Genetic engineering may lead to cures for such diseases as cystic fibrosis and even some cancers. New technology may hold the secret of how to finally reverse the chain reaction that led to global warming. Scientists are trying to develop devices called fuel cells that will use hydrogen extracted from water as clean energy. Nuclear scientists want to create energy from nuclear fusion, the kind of atomic reactions that occur on the sun. A nuclear fusion reaction could provide the energy to operate electric power plants and do it without generating radioactive waste. Improvements in devices called solar cells could capture part of the enormous energy coming directly from the sun.

New technologies also may set off environmental chain reactions. Many choices will need to be made that weigh the benefits against the risks. Citizens can help by being well informed about genetic engineering, global warming, and other environ-

Solar cells capture energy from the sun and convert it into electricity; batteries can be used to store power for use at night or on cloudy days.

mental issues. Learning about new energy sources is a good place to start. Many decisions will need to be made about ways to reverse harmful environmental chain reactions and keep new ones from starting. Voters and political leaders need to gather all the information they can to make good choices about the future of our planet.

1830s
Charles Darwin concludes that species evolve through competition for resources

1896
Swedish chemist and physicist Svante Arrhenius links changes in climate to changes in amounts of carbon dioxide in the atmosphere

1920s
Vladimir Ivanovich Vernadsky discovers that living things put carbon dioxide, nitrogen, and oxygen gases into the atmosphere

1935
British biologist Sir Arthur George Tansley coins the term *ecology* and begins its study as a science

1953
Biologists discover the structure of DNA, the molecule genes are made of

1962
Rachel Carson's book, *Silent Spring*, warns of pollution dangers to the environment, especially the effects of the pesticide DDT

1963
National Academy of Sciences warns that the greenhouse effect could lead to rising sea levels

1968
Scientists invent genetic engineering techniques for splicing a gene from one organism into the DNA of another

1970s
Scientists prove that phosphorus pollution causes lake eutrophication

1975
Scientists help write laws that begin the cleanup of acid rain

1985
British meteorologists discover that a hole has formed in the ozone layer over Antarctica

1994
U.S. Food and Drug Administration approves the first genetically engineered food plant, a tomato

2006
Biologists find an alien shrimp species from Eastern Europe living in the Great Lakes

2007
United Nations scientific panel concludes that human activities caused increased carbon dioxide levels leading to global warming

2008
The World Wildlife Fund releases a report estimating that wildlife diversity has decreased by 25 percent over the past 35 years

TIMELINE

GLOSSARY

algae
plantlike organisms that live mostly in water

atmosphere
blanket of gases that surrounds a planet

bacteria
single-celled microscopic creatures that exist everywhere in nature

biome
large area on Earth containing certain types of plants

carbon
chemical element found in all living things and forming the basis for life

carbon dioxide
gas in the air that animals give off and plants use to make food; greenhouse gas in air that traps heat from the sun

decomposers
organisms, usually bacteria or fungi, that break down dead plants and animals into simpler substances

DNA
molecule of which genes are made

ecosystem
all of the living and nonliving parts of a particular area

eutrophication
dense plant growth caused by too many nutrients, eventually killing animal life

fertilizer
substances, such as manure or chemicals, to make soil richer and better for growing crops

fragmentation
breaking up into separate pieces

gene
basic unit of heredity

habitat
area within an ecosystem where a group of the same kind of organisms lives at the same time

mercury
poisonous chemical element given off by burning certain fossil fuels

niche
role a population plays in an ecosystem

oxygen
gas that plants and animals need for life but that is also given off as a waste product when plants produce food

petroleum
oil, a liquid fossil fuel

phosphorus
chemical element and nutrient for plants

plankton
tiny one-celled animals and algae

toxin
poison

FURTHER RESOURCES

ON THE WEB

For more information on this topic, use FactHound.

1. Go to *www.facthound.com*
2. Type in this book ID: 0756539498
3. Click on the *Fetch It* button.

FactHound will find the best Web sites for you.

FURTHER READING

Drake, Jane, Ann Love, and Mark Thurman. *Alien Invaders: Species That Threaten Our World*. Toronto: Tundra Books, 2008.

Gray, Susan H. *Food Webs: Interconnecting Food Chains*. Minneapolis: Compass Point Books, 2008.

Simpson, Kathleen. *National Geographic Investigates: Extreme Weather: Science Tackles Global Warming and Climate Change*. Washington, D.C.: National Geographic Children's Books, 2008.

Sivertsen, Linda, and Tosh Sivertsen. *Generation Green: The Ultimate Teen Guide to Living an Eco-Friendly Life*. New York: Simon Pulse, 2008.

Trueit, Trudi Strain. *The Water Cycle*. Danbury Conn.: Franklin Watts, 2002.

LOOK FOR OTHER BOOKS IN THIS SERIES:

Climate Crisis: The Science of Global Warming

Cure Quest: The Science of Stem Cell Research

Goodbye, Gasoline: The Science of Fuel Cells

Great Shakes: The Science of Earthquakes

Rise of the Thinking Machines: The Science of Robots

SOURCE NOTES

Chapter 1: "Sludge Recycling Sends Antiseptic Soap Ingredient to Agriculture." Johns Hopkins Bloomberg School of Public Health. 26 April 2006. 21 April 2008. www.jhsph.edu/publichealthnews/press_releases/2006/halden_sludge.html

Chapter 2: "Habitat Destruction May Wipe Out Monarch Butterfly Migration." Science Daily. 5 April 2008. 15 May 2008. www.sciencedaily.com/releases/2008/04/080401230705.htm

Chapter 3: "Shrimpy Invaders." Science News for Kids. 17 Jan. 2007. 21 April 2008. www.sciencenewsforkids.org/articles/20070117/Note2.asp

Chapter 4: Carolyn Marshall. "Oil Spill Spreads in San Francisco Bay." *The New York Times*. 10 Nov. 2007. 21 April 2008. www.nytimes.com/2007/11/10/us/10spill.html

Chapter 5: Matthew L. Wald. "Study Details How U.S. Could Cut 28% of Greenhouse Gases." *The New York Times*. 30 Nov. 2007. 21 April 2008. www.nytimes.com/2007/11/30/business/30green.html

Chapter 6: "Genetically Engineered Corn May Harm Stream Ecosystems." National Science Foundation. 10 Oct. 2007. 21 April 2008. www.eurekalert.org/pub_releases/2007-10/nsf-gec101007.php

ABOUT THE AUTHOR

Darlene R. Stille is a science writer and author of more than 80 books for young people. She grew up in Chicago and attended the University of Illinois, where she discovered her love of writing. She has received numerous awards for her work. She lives and writes in Michigan.

INDEX